PowerKids Readers:

Big Cats

LIONS

Elizabeth Vogel

The Rosen Publishing Group's
PowerKids Press™
New York

Published in 2002 by The Rosen Publishing Group, Inc.
29 East 21st Street, New York, NY 10010

First Edition

Book Design: Michael Donnellan

Photo Credits: pp. 1, 7, 9, 16, 17 © Digital Vision; pp. 5, 15, 19, 21 © Mark Newman; p. 11 © Andre Hote/International Stock.

Vogel, Elizabeth.
Lions / Elizabeth Vogel.— 1st ed.
    p. cm. — (Big cats)
ISBN 0-8239-6021-8 (lib. bdg.)
1. Lions—Juvenile literature. [1. Lions.] I. Title.
QL737.C23 V637 2002
599.757—dc21
                                                    00-013007

Manufactured in the United States of America

CONTENTS

1 Kings of the Jungle   4

2 Lions Live in a Pride   12

3 Words to Know   22

4 Books and Web Sites   23

5 Index   24

6 Word Count   24

7 Note   24

Lions are big cats.
Lions sometimes are
called the kings of
the jungle. They
are very mighty.

5

Lions are one of the largest of the big cats. Only tigers are bigger.

7

Lions have golden fur. The male lion has a mane.

A mane is thick, golden or brown fur around a lion's head. Male lions are the only cats that have manes.

Lions live in a special family called a pride. The pride lives together in the wild.

Some lions live in
parks or zoos.

Lions like to eat meat.
They eat antelope and
zebra.

Both female and male
lions hunt for meat. They
hunt when it is dark
outside. This helps them
surprise the antelope.

A baby lion is called a cub. Lion cubs learn how to hunt from their mothers.

21

WORDS TO KNOW

antelope

cub

mane

pride

Here are more books to read about lions:
The Big Cats: Lions and Tigers and Leopards
by Jennifer Urquehart
National Geographic Society

Lions
by Don Middleton
Rosen Publishing

To learn more about lions, check out these Web sites:
http://dialspace.dial.pipex.com/agarman/
        bco/ver4.htm
www.discovery.com

INDEX

A

antelope, 16, 18

C

cats, 4, 6, 10

cub, 20

F

female, 18

fur, 8, 10

H

hunt, 18, 20

J

jungle, 4

M

male, 8, 10, 18

mane, 8, 10

meat, 16, 18

P

pride, 12

T

tigers, 6

Z

zebra, 16

Word Count: 133

Note to Librarians, Teachers, and Parents

PowerKids Readers are specially designed to help emergent and beginning readers build their skills in reading for information. Simple vocabulary and concepts are paired with stunning, detailed images from the natural world around them. Readers will respond to written language by linking meaning with their own everyday experiences and observations. Sentences are short and simple, employing a basic vocabulary of sight words, as well as new words that describe objects or processes that take place in the natural world. Large type, clean design, and photographs corresponding directly to the text all help children to decipher meaning. Features such as a contents page, picture glossary, and index help children to get the most out of PowerKids Readers. They also introduce children to the basic elements of a book, which they will encounter in their future reading experiences. Lists of related books and Web sites encourage kids to explore other sources and to continue the process of learning.

DEC 2001

GAYLORD M